Once Upon a Time in Never Never Land

Once in Upon a Time in Never Never Land

ADDICTS BEWARE

AMELIA HATHOW

ISBN: 978-1-958150-94-8
Once Upon A Time In Never Never Land: Addicts Beware

Paperpack
September 2022

Subjects:
PSYCHOLOGY / Psychopathology / Addiction
SELF-HELP / Substance Abuse & Addictions / Alcohol
PSYCHOLOGY / Interpersonal Relations

ameliahathow.com

You are dedicating your new life

to the very ONE who

means the most, YOU.

Table of Contents

Introduction

This is a book about drugs, health, and your ultimate direction. We will speak of life's lessons and the ending result of saturated feelings. Saturated feelings are what is causing the addictions that are running rampant. Not the drugs themselves. Saturated feelings are the HOOK, so to speak. And why wouldn't it be? It's not the actual drugs doing it ALL. IT'S the feelings gained by those types of drugs. A clear sign that people just WANT to FEEL more of life. There is really nothing seriously wrong with THAT NEED until it starts killing people. THEN IT IS A CLEAR ISSUE AT HAND FOR ALL.

An "apostle" is nothing more than a "man" or "woman" who happened to be next to someone who actually meant something to all else. All else, meaning, US. Your persuaders and influencers. Influenced by the same drug of choice, freedom. But true freedom never rains down like it does now, half knowing what a real "high" is. A "high" so high that one truly needs to be pulled down from it, literally. As when an apostle starts to live his or her life, he or she thinks so highly of his or her purpose. Yet, they all die the same plight, of no one really knowing who he or she was. That is because he or she will live a life of not being known until thousands of years later. High upon everyone else's pedestal thinking he or she has something important to reveal. Yet, no one ever truly listens anyways. By the time his or her real message is understood others are dying from a high. Why is that so, you mangy monsters ask? Because they too reap their sowing needle stuck into their arms.

Dissatisfaction with LIFE itself. This is the name of the game. Satisfaction and dissatisfaction. Nothing more, nothing less. It all boils down to whether one can BE SATISFIED WITHOUT ANYTHING IN ONE'S MOUTH OR GULLET DESPITE ONE'S WELL BEING. We know the sensation of being high or what not, giving one's emotions never felt before. But the after effects are tremendous compared to not putting anything into any part of your body in any fashion whether intravenously or through your mouths. It's all the same concept. One addiction is no worse than the other. Take this eater for example, who likes to eat an outrageous amount of potato chips in one sitting. That's fine. But in the long haul of it all, those chips' contents will leave traces of fat all over their body to be consumed by God itself. Yes, God eats what you eat. It consumes what you consume because it is inside of almost every living organelle in you, and it goes without saying that there are some that IT is NOT in. And which ones are these, exactly? That is a very curious question, right? Which organelles is our God not IN, exactly? Well, to be clear, these are the cells that don't have anything IN them to begin with. And which ones would they be, right? A shell of a cell with no content. You can't know this until you dive further into your own self. Get it yet? We can't come right out and tell you these things unless you actually strive to understand yourselves first.

FOR FUTURE ENDEAVORS
BEHOLD OH WRECK'D ADDICTS

Let's begin by describing our effects on those who have any kind of addiction, such as most people who are breathing. We aren't allowed to put any extra emphasis on someone's pains from addiction. But we ARE allowed to keep enticing someone to their breaking point. From our standpoint there isn't anyone who really isn't addicted to something. Instead of thinking you are addicted, just think of it as an extreme usage of whatever your intense usage is WITH. Therefore relieving any implications that you or anyone else is actually addicted to ANYTHING. Intensity of focus to use something is way far more forgiving than someone thinking they are always going to be an addict, a word that is being thrown around way too much. And this is coming from someone who WAS a real addict, or so I thought, the king himself, Elvis Presley. Yup. It's me. In the flesh. Once again to speak on behalf of all of us who are still living amongst your dead. I say this in response to those who still carry that addict mentality. Death is your only salvation from such a stigma placed on you by someone who was already self deprecating. So, be very careful with carrying on this lineage of a self appointed "addict." It won't carry you to your next level of relief, EVER. The ONLY ACTUAL relief you will ever get is from wiping away that stigma placed onto you from someone else's idea. You are your own label maker. Make a new label for yourself that best describes what you are actually going through instead of being labeled an addict, so others can grab ahold of your soul forever. As one addict to the next, I started to label myself something quite remarkably different, after death. Yes, I am still holding on to those addict ideas. They follow you even after life, the physical kind, that is. So, someone of similar abilities and talents, giving me advice, started to show me a word that may suit me better besides: addict. Frompulous. Yes. That's it. What is this exactly, right? A new word to describe what is actually happening beyond our grave wherever we end up. Fromping along like dead deer in the headlights look. And then bam. You're dead again. Not from sobriety, but from feeling so free we all end up running in front of another vehicle like my friend did when she finally got sober. Does anyone know of whom I am speaking? Of course not. Because their death hasn't happened yet. My sister in law. Of all people, she was the one to point me in another direction besides calling me an addict. She severely understood the real implications of labeling others. For she was called so many names by yours truly that it backfired on to me. My addiction reeled its ugly head then I collapsed from pure exhaustion. It really wasn't the medication that killed me. It was neglecting my "self." A common occurrence where we are looking from, down below, into the trenches of it all. Right beneath your faces. Not so close to purgatory, but there is a level beneath our faces that keeps us from looking into our "selves" just like the ones in purgatory. It's not quite as harsh but the real pain begins when you are reborn again just like a crack addicted baby. The pains still arise even when one is reincarnated as I am about to do, once again, at my discomfort. I will be born in a time of utmost chaos. Till this day is born you all are going to experience something not that many of our kind too often go through. You see, God has been feeling our addictions, too, and also has become one. Addicted to every kind of addict that we have wanted to become regardless of kind. Now it grows tired of it all. The addicted feelings, that is. So, it will replenish itself once again just like it has done so many other times. But, this time there will be recordings and videos of this event(s) because IT will cause this replenishment over and over until IT is no longer addicted as well, to the feeling of it (addiction). We did this to IT. God that is. And now it is time to pay.

Blessed Be My Lord and Savior, My "SELF"

Elvis P

Elvis P:

We will be summoned right after each of our deaths and will have to confess to WHY we became addicts for whichever type we are – which are so numerous; addiction isn't quite as understood as a lot of people thought. Addiction to music is also an addiction. If one continuously listens to music just to hear a particular sound or beat, over and over again, in order to feel a particular way, that is addiction. Addiction comes in so many forms. The Bible is also an addiction. Being so enticed and enthralled with a book is also an addiction. This has been happening for way too long in so many ways that something must be done, a start over on a grand scale. So get ready, for IT is growing restless, experiencing a needed fix to grab onto, the death of all of us once and for all. That is what it takes to end an addiction. To wipe it all away clean and begin again, fresh and clean like a brand new summer rain falling from ITs eyes onto a fresh empty earth with no one to pollute it anymore. Sorry to be the bearer of seemingly bad news. But this train wreck will also die an early death as soon as I am born. This is one of my lessons in life, to die very quickly without knowing even what real addiction doesn't lead to, a true death. A more pure death. Try that out for size. Clean yourself up before it all gets wiped away, clean, and you may be spared the horrificness that will follow. For all of you supposed addicts, rename yourself as quickly as possible. Relieve yourself of such a label, a burden, no doubt. YOU DEFINE YOUR LIFE FROM NOW ON. NO ONE

ELSE. Can you try that on for size? Not to be more abrupt, but time is not on your side. IT will replenish its skins two summers from this year and this will be an event to bear witness to.

Loving kindness makes your/our addiction worse.

Elvis, With Regards to ALL

This is someone who has been crack addicted even after death because those needs are still with me today as we type through this man's hands who are just as addicted to the keys as I was to that pipe and crack pebble sized candy rock. I say candy for that is what it was. My language has been twisted in reflection of such a sweet smoke being inhaled by my lustful lungs. I was never lustful at all. In fact, I was merely trying to get to a place. A place far far away from what I was actually never wanting to experience, life itself. In the name of God, the Almighty, that is what this addiction is all about. Any addiction. Not wanting to face the truth of it all. That we are not and never will be anything other than what you experience in the flesh. No amount of drugs will keep you from being what God and every other being wants you to be: nothing at all. This is going to be a reiteration until everyone gets this idea into their bodies. No amount of drugs or any other addictive thing will keep you from experiencing this nothingness. In fact, over time, it will be unnecessarily put upon you until you realize that you are nothing but dirt trying to grasp for light from the sun itself.

You will be made to know that you are so low in the dirt that climbing your way up will be your only option. While you are climbing, every one of your breaths will be that of God's, suppressing your very soul down into nothingness because that is where IT is headed, too. In a blink of an eye IT will flash itself with fire burning all that has rebuked IT's very existence. A cleansing like no other. For those of you who haven't paid attention to your "self" much, this will be a rude awakening. The smoke will burn from your insides out, depleting you of all extraordinary addictions. Your cleansing won't be soft by any means. This harshness of your truth to your addictions will only burn that much brighter, faster, and with so much heat your internal skins won't melt, but just flash fire in you, making you burn from the inside out. Of all the orifcies you have, you will most likely bleed hot blood along with your melted bowels coming out of your anal cavity. I call it cavity because a burning hole will melt around and dissolve your anus engulfing all that is near it. Good luck and don't take this personally. Even this writer has a few addictions to tackle before the end becomes truth to ALL.

You will never guess who this may be talking through a simple little peon of a man such as this one typing away for those who he can't even see. But he has something you don't, a drive. A direction of some kind. At least this writer knows his end to come and it isn't going to be a very nice way to go. See yourself doing something other than trying to feel anything anymore. Disengage with those who only fuel your fire to feel anything at all, even love for that matter. Because that is what is destroying you on the inside out. Not unconditional love, but the love that people profess they have for you when they keep saying you are something that you are not. It is so easy to label yourself something so you can continue on the same road of being someone who is only temporarily fixed by something that will always exist – addiction itself. You see, people misunderstand that absolutely everyone is an addict of some sort. This is going to be a shock to everyone who reads this, but you are only an "addict" if you claim yourself to be one. Once you do that you stop actual growth out of being an extremist because that is all addiction is. Going to an extreme towards anything even professing one's love for God itself. God doesn't want others to revere it, only to move in a direction that inspires growth. Labeling yourself forever doesn't inspire anything but stagnation and revolting thoughts towards oneself on a continual basis. Another addiction. Labeling oneself only promotes addiction to that very thing that you will eventually become. You see, over time, any label that is put upon you whether it came from you or anyone else becomes a living thing on you. Thus, becoming a permanent fix onto your "self." Think about this as you go along with your programs to always be something forever. That is not life. You go against the very fabric of life which is constant change. Do you understand what I am saying yet? YOU ARE FIGHTING AGAINST NATURE BY NOT LETTING GO OF OTHER PEOPLE'S IDEAS ABOUT HOW THEY WANT TO LIVE. You are an individual by nature. Look in a mirror and see your differences. Once you can grasp that you were meant to experience differently, you won't place someone else's label onto your own living being. Try it once. Relabel yourself something other than an addict of any kind. Name it, "Extremist." Name it, "Forever Indulging in the naughty for now until I am no longer in desire of it." Whatever you want. But don't label yourself something that becomes a permanent part of your very core. That is destruction in and of itself. Be fluid. Be kind to others who claim to know it all and want to process your ideals into a meat grinder only to be used up by the very animals that only want for your ideals to be wiped away clean. Only to serve their needs as a self-indulgent aristocrat who wants nothing more than to wallow in his own sorrow with others. That is exactly what labeling yourself with such a label does. Causes only more addiction to THAT LABEL. That very label that is keeping you from stepping out of hindrance.

Well, time to drink up or shoot up or pop those pills while you can. Soon and we mean very soon a flash of lights will appear from our skies. They will not be a friendly "light." So many lights will appear that you and everyone else will think it is the stars coming screaming at you like a spark of light from your cigarette piped, once lit, too many times, causing such abrasive actions against itself IT won't even know when and where or who or why. Does this make sense to you? It shouldn't because it was you talking when you were high in those days of late and the near future crawling forward, on your belly trying to get to safety when it all happens. Now is your time to really start grasping what we are trying to convey to you. You may be hooked on something, drug of choice, or not, but one day all of that will disappear in such a quick storyline across your skies that the best drug dealers won't even have time to breathe God's last breath before they know they are burnt to a crisp just like what they have been doing to their buyers, burning their inside souls out. Truth be told, we don't really want to write a book for people who are so strung out on that very word, addiction, that we are almost telling this writer to just scrap what she/he has written so far. But why keep you addicts out of our plan when we aren't even keeping serial killers and future serial killers out of our plan? Why do you all need the most help? Do you ever ask for anything else besides money to buy drugs? Not really. Food sometimes. Only when you are really hungry and need food to survive in order to get your next hit. So, why do we still pursue trying to convince others like yourselves that there is another way to approach life that IS REALLY HARD TO LIVE THROUGH ESPECIALLY IN THESE TOUGH TIMES? Which, by the way, you created yourselves over many lifetimes just like your sons and daughters have and their children to be, unless we wipe their little bodies and minds out, too. For too long so many of you addicts have been prying into other people's lives in order to get what will never relieve any pain from anything that will happen to you or that has happened. Oh, and believe me, what is coming ahead for the likes of you all, addict or not, is so extreme before your fresh eyeballs that weeping won't even come close to what people will do when they figure out their time on earth is close to an end. We have been writing about this for decades upon decades upon iterations of so many years that finally we are able to convince someone that this will come true. Are you one of them? You should be. Because if your addicted bodies can withstand such controversy from the inside out it won't be such a big deal to witness the burning fire rolling down upon you. There really will be no difference because that junk you fill your minds and souls with only causes your fire to burn even hotter inside out. The very carbon that dies off last actually flames up when you begin to destroy your mind and body like every addict does when they inject whatever makes them feel better. Believe us when we say this to you all, start giving it all up. Every addictive remedy you have all made. Once and for all. Read the Corinthians if you are a Bible reader. Read Revelations if you seek destruction rather than growth. They are coming to fruition very soon. But there is something that both the Bible and the Quran will never mention. We, your older siblings, your beloved little big eyed, scrawny aliens ARE

YOUR RULERS. Read Ephesians 6:10 -18. That is exactly who we are and the arrows we speak of when we refer to any sort of fire coming down upon you. IT IS HAPPENING IN LESS THAN TWO YEARS TIME. Approximately in the summer months of 2024. Why is it not so specific anymore? Because you all can actually change the when. When that Ephesian event will happen. YOU ALL DO THIS BY BEING HOPEFUL FOR YOUR FUTURE. The trick is: more hope. The length of time extends before we unleash the Ephesian arrows upon your lands, seas, homes, animal livestock and yourselves, including your little lambs (Your Beloved Child(ren)). We really do not care too much about who gets these arrows and why. We were forced to do this from your intentions towards each other. That is how it works. It is a build up of attitudes and physical intentions towards each other that builds this desire from you to US, your elders. Your Elder Siblings.

Don't be scared. Be mindful of what you all have done to yourselves. Be responsible for things that added up over time and will cause such massive destruction. The skins of God will peel away all of your sinful ways, the addicts included. Peeling away from blasts that will happen from those Ephesian arrows. We tell you this to get you ready for what kind of preparation you all can do to stay alive. Even the sinners can be spared if and only if they take us seriously. However, and we don't say this too often for gratuitous sake, those who have walked the earth at that moment of destruction, regardless of where you are at, will not be spared one inch. All of you will be ripped, torn, and strewn about like slaughtered lambs from a spring rain, raining down bullets upon them so speedily, the speed alone destroys the very fabric of their scientific proof that they do exist, but no more, because of us child killers, too. Just like the Uvalde shooter who was only following our plan for our sake alone. There will be another one to follow that will make Uvalde look like a merry-go-round full of happy children instead of a gymnasium full of slaughtered lambs, bloodied so with sooooo many holes in them that even swiss cheese would take a second glance to make sure they were not being remade into a red piece of slaughtered lambs whose fleece will always be stained with jealousy. Go to your loved ones now, you addicts of all kinds, and remember this: only those who truly start to BEGIN a better understanding of why they are here on this planet might get a better life the next time they are reborn into another addict's body. Either way, you WILL return AS AN ADDICT, OVER AND OVER AGAIN. The same as those shooters who will kill more and more children at our request and persuasions. And why would we do such a thing? To get your attention to the power of US, YOUR ACTUAL RULERS. Once you are convinced of our role in your lives then and only then will we start to create some relief on your lives. Until then you will reap and sow, reap and sow, reap and sow until nothing is left for anyone to be addicted to. Not even your televisions. Even now all of you barely take time to read such filth such as this book because you are so addicted to someone else's life rather than fixing yours. The Kardasians are a prime example of how a family can be such an attraction for so many other lives that they don't even consider the repercussions of creating such a show only to bury people in their own filthy ways without giving them a chance to try and work on their own issues. And yes, that was a choice for those viewers, but if everyone could understand the limited time everyone has, then no one would even glance at such a scandalous creation. C'est la vie. Right? What's done is done. No going back. Especially in your predicament. So many people living vicariously through television. Zooming together to try and create relationships that will only last as quickly as the time it took to turn their laptops on. Who else is going to turn your head besides a writer who could care less of what happens to him? Yes, he chose to be a pawn to make sure these little books are spread across the world as much as he possibly can before it all comes burning down. Addicts you are. Only because someone decided to create such a word to best describe their own demise and self-deprecation THEY WANTED TO LIVE IN EVEN AFTER THEY STOPPED DOING ALL OF THEIR ADDICTIVE HABITS. And it wasn't just cocaine or alcohol. What about their desire to put others in their own shoes? To make people live what and how THEY wanted to experience THEIR life, not yours. Do you ever wonder if that person asked anyone else for a better way to get over someone else's addiction? No. They convinced so many others that their programs can work for everyone. How can that be when your designs, at every level, IS DIFFERENT and was specifically designed for your own issues to conquer in your own way and NOT from someone else's way? Who are they to create such an authoritative program for people who are different in almost every single aspect? Creation begins when everyone realizes that THEY can create FOR THEIR OWN DESIGN given to them by US, not God. In particular, your soul and spirit. Let me clue you all in on something. The names given to those two entities I just mentioned, soul and spirit, are only names. They are not actually anything but a programmed hologram. Boom. A programmed hologram that is attached to your bodies. Yes, attached. And yes, bodies. Your physical body is combined with your actual "ghostly" self. We are telling you all this because your physical world, despite its density, is only a highly dense reflection. And yes, we do understand it is extremely dense and how could a reflection be sooooo dense? That is a great question to ask. But, you are missing the point as we missed explaining your ghostly body versus the more dense one you all are convinced that is actually you. Haha. The movie The Matrix almost got it right. Instead of something feeding you nutrients to keep your body alive, it is the other way around. We feed your body with food for thought. Because it is your mind that ACTUALLY keeps you and your ghostly body alive which are combined in such a way that a mist wouldn't even come close to describing how thin your actual ghostly body is. Ethereal material IS NOT the material of your ghostly body. But your soul and spirit are. Your ghostly body is actually behind you. You should see this writer's eyes perk up because something dawned on him recently which he will write about later. Or should we say WE will make him write about him and his specific recent findings. Anyways, your ghostly image is attached to your spine. People have called it names such as a Kundalini type of energy but Kundalini is only a part of their ghostly body. Kundalini is actually their innards if ghosts HAD innards. It is quite complicated, really. So, let us try to explain it in simpler terms. Your thick body, and we have to keep emphasizing thick because it is and there is no denying that fact, is being projected out like a TV screen. Yes. I said it. A television screen. Or better yet, a projector image from a seed of sorts. And yes, just from a little seed. It's weird, but what this little seed IS is a massive amount of energy rolled into many many many, and we keep needing to say many, layers of images of you over and over again. It is like rolling a piece of dough over itself so many times that eventually, no matter how you roll it, it becomes, always, projected as a piece of dough, regardless of who is rolling it. And that is another projection to consider. Who rolled you into that projection? The seed, we mean. Who rolled that seed, over and over again, so many thousands of times it becomes what you see in the mirror and in someone else's sunglasses? A reflection you are.

So, let's get back to addiction.

Addiction to anything is a significant problem. Once you are hooked into anything with meaningless outcomes you will destroy everything that you come across, even your own family and friends. Why does such a phenomenon happen? We still don't know why. But we can tell you that we WILL make everyone some sort of addict to get them to learn how to use their MIND to get out of whatever extreme focus they ventured onto. And it is only an extremity. Nothing is ever so addicting that you can't stop from needing it or desiring it. That's just plain failure to understand the true nature of your mind. That's all. A severe misunderstanding of your own mind's capabilities. Nothing more, nothing less. We tell you this because this time we want to change everyone's outlet for everyone else needing to cling onto a description of someone else's plights and severe misunderstanding of themselves. Addicts are nothing more than those who don't have a clear understanding of THE mind, an everadapting phenomena that so many others have used to solve so many more difficult problems besides continuously putting something in them to get a feeling of escape because that is all they are doing. And that you are doing, if you still think you are an addict. Trust us with this. WE are your creators besides what God has created alone. Afterwards, WE started to change everything else on our own. And WE are so very in tune with your design because we are the fractal of your source, in particular.

Now the bad news... An awakening is occurring amongst several millions. And we say millions because the actual count is unpredictable at each moment just like the ones who WILL COMMIT themselves to a new way. A new way of seeing US. We will not be something good to look at. WE are, in fact, not anything significant, as far as in terms of beauty. Our "looks" resemble the very ones that were portrayed in the movie about HIM. Tom. His name is irrelevant. But we will give you a first name to get you ready for his movie to come that will show our true reveals. He will produce a movie forced by our minds, not his at all. You will know when this movie comes out to be seen by ALL. This is not so cryptic to give you ALL a chance to get ready for our introduction, physically. This WILL happen. His movie is going to be about OUR ultimate deconstruction of our creation, your lives from near start to finish. Beneath the surface his filmology has always revolved around our push to make you see us in a very stark light. Our intentions towards you ALL is to give you as much to experience in the shortest amount of time as possible. There are other plans for some of you who HAVE to be put through hardships. The plan doesn't matter, but getting through what is shoved down your gullets does. Time should never be spent wondering what our plan will be because it is always in a sort of flux anyways. That can't be helped. And that is why it is a total waste of time wondering about our plans with you ALL. Just know that there is order and some sense to our decisions about where we want you to be in and at.

Peace is never an issue as long as ALL just agree on something big enough to pull everyone together. We hold ourselves responsible for the mayhem that is being thrown at you. Right now, in your years, regardless of your religious years, it will always be a game for OUR playing to figure out what is best, not for any of you but for the bigger picture. Producing a species that is willing to work hard for OUR end goals. And when we say OUR, on this matter, we mean ALL of us, including you all too. We are not totally without empathy for we have been through just as hard a life as you will be going through. So, we know what exactly you will be going through. Not only have we gone through these same hardships as you but the only reason we are able to create such hardships for you is because we have built programs, artificial programs to make you go through. Yes, they are artificial programs. Some of your movies that portray you all living in some sort of alternate reality is partially true. More so towards a creation that has a living mind in it at the same time. Someone will portray this very thing pretty soon by OUR will towards this person. His name has already been mentioned. It is NOT Cruise. Another Tom. Not to say he can't, but there is another Tom who has been our motion picture slave for a long time. People, or we should point out, some people have created a decent following around him. So far, some people are taking his film history seriously. Not seriously enough for anyone to think he is being told to write his messages down like this writer is now. Both of them are in total slavery to us. This writer is fairly new to our Mastery over him. Tom is not. He is a much older man about to breathe his last breath. So look for his filmology if you want to really know what is going on with you and how you are and will live for a long time to come.

Choices are made, real choices, that is, when your "self" can distinguish between your real agenda as someone living temporarily on this earth. On a planet with such enormous proportions, people tend to forget the actual growth this earth has made throughout its own lifetime, which has been a very very very long time unlike yours comparatively. Remember this, choose to be smart or die trying. "Smartness" is also relatively new to your kind. In fact, your intelligence has only been around for maybe a million or so years, not enough to boast about compared to all other intelligences that have grown far and beyond even around you. Meaning, all the earthly vegetation you see are much much older than you all. Yet, you destroy them so flippantly and carelessly as if your species owns the rights to do so. You do not. In fact, WE own those rights. Yet, you still deny this reality. Your addictions prevent you ALL from seeing US in your skies. Unfortunately, OUR truth will reign hell upon you because it will be such a shock that people will run for cover knowing why we are here. In time, you ALL, when being born again will have a very distinct feeling that you are lower than any life form around you. We will make this feeling so engrained deeply that killing yourself will be your first inclination. But, by doing so will only bring that feeling back much stronger as you are reborn again and again and again. Killing yourself should never be your first option when things don't go your way. However, and we don't really like to say that, we do understand this need to just want to end it all not really knowing IF you will have another go at life again, yet hoping you don't because the life you just left was and should have been horrible on all accounts. You did this to your "self," by the way. Plus, a little help from us to get you to that breaking point. WE DO NOT CARE AT ALL whether you off yourself. WE DO CARE whether you are trying to live though because THAT IS THE POINT OF IT ALL. TO LIVE ANOTHER DAY AND PUSH ALONG WITH ALL OF YOUR MIGHT. THAT IS WHEN WE DECIDE THAT YOU DESERVE A BREAK IN LIFE. But, WE won't intervene until WE are absolutely sure you are ready for real change. Until then, WE will keep feeding you addictive tendencies until you are so low that you put the final death sentence in your grips. One way or another WE will destroy every tendency you have for bad and exponentially make it all so bad that your only direction is destroying everything around you as God is going to do very soon now. Why, you ask? Because the addictions are so rampant that God is no longer growing anymore. It too is spiraling down into the dwells of your kind.

IT too is feeling so depressed that it is about to kill IT "self" from the sheer feeling of not wanting to live anymore. WE and YOU have been doing this TO IT for TOO LONG. So, IT is going to repel ALL these addictive tendencies back to cleanliness. The difference between IT and US is its ability to just cleanse IT "self" without even considering others. Oh wait. That is exactly what WE do as well. WE don't even consider what we are doing to ourselves impacts God itself. Yes, your behaviors have been impacting the very fabric OF God. Because YOU and WE are part of its fabric.

Too many addicts all rolled up into their little communities thriving and diving into that same little community. So many of you reliving those days, in your own minds, behind each other's backs, deeply regretting every step you took up until that moment you "became" sober. Yet sobriety will only be a term used by, still, addicts, to this day, addicted to that very community, only to strive for perfection. Maybe perfection isn't the right word to use to describe your attempts to "stay" sober. Maybe another word needs to be invented to steer you away from where you have been going. Maybe someone else beside the person who created this ridiculous program can create a word that steers people into a better direction besides reliving those past moments of horribly creating a life that brought everyone down with it including your fucking God. Yes, you heathens who always and still do think only of your fucking sobriety never would have guessed that what you are still doing keeps God down in the pits of your neverending, relentless pursuit of being someone who someone else wanted to be: a clear thinking person, once again. Because that is what this is really about. Thinking cleanly, not "being" clean. "Thinking" is the only last thing you will ever do when you take your last breath. Thinking your way out of all the bad decisions you made before you became dead. Steer clear of those who think THEY know best. Only you do. Once and for all, clean your mind of all those ideas that make you stagnant. Put into a position that keeps you positioned as one thing or one "type" of person. That stagnation idea goes against "how" actual life and God works, one in the same. God is your life always dying inside and outside, never the same, just like the cells that you have been rapidly killing over and over again only to come to find out that all you have been doing is killing God's innards more quickly then IT wanted you to do. No big deal, IT can keep up with whatever you bring across ITs plane of existence only to make you a Master of your own will. But, remember, days will come when IT will have to relinquish those unnecessary cells that keep rapidly being killed off over and over again. IT doesn't know what or who is actually doing this killing at a rapid pace. IT only knows that a segment of IT has an issue just like the cells inside YOUR body that reacts to something foreign or unusual, they attack it or atleast try to heal them. Eventually, those cells will be disposed of one way or another just like what you do to God, being disposed of yourself, one way or another. You see, IT too fights back in ITs own way to relieve itself of continuous and unusual activities within IT and out of IT. You will eventually become something to be disposed of at a rapid pace unless you decide to change your mind about this whole scheme of things. You will have no mercy upon you at all, from anyone. You are your own keeper, no one else. No one here gives two shits about who, what, how, why, or when you have ever been. Keep this in mind when you keep deciding to follow someone else's idea that only keeps you on death's door. God doesn't care either way. Either design your own way out, cleanly thinking your way out of old ideas or continuously die like the addict you will always be, now and forever, a million years long.

Keep going with your relentless pursuits of unhappiness. This WILL come across as a book that will ALWAYS be rude and harsh. IT needs to be done. NO ONE HAS THE BALLS TO SCREAM WHAT HAS TO BE SAID, YOU GUYS ARE IDIOTS FOR ALWAYS FOLLOWING HIS PLAN. HIS PLAN, NOT YOURS. Why do you think you are different in every way? Why? Why? Why? Because you WERE MEANT to steer your own course, IN your OWN way, you fucking idiot.

Always know that there are elements of Truth IN you. How is that possible? In the first place, you are part of God and

God IS all things including truth. So, somewhere INSIDE lies truth. That being said, stop thinking about HOW to get out of someone else's mannerisms or causes only to find your way into yours. WE know that didn't make sense, but neither does the way you have been living your life to BECOME something that you have always been: clear in thought, clear in mind. THAT IS THE ABSOLUTE TRUTH. The trick is to STOP thinking so much and over-simplify everything. Yes, break down all that is happening to you in little segments. See where the root cause leads to. That is what and where you NEED to work on. It will be so small that getting there will take forever, sometimes. Not a problem. What you really should be concerned about is when.

Go ahead and stop reading if you want. We know this is a lot to take in all at once. But, in the end, those programs will cease to exist just like everything else. Change is coming for you no matter what. So, it is better to be prepared to meet US in clear minded thinking before it all comes crashing, spiraled down, into it ALL, US, your judges. WE will judge you on behalf of IT because IT can't judge from ITs position. It's impossible for something to judge when it keeps everything glued together. That has been the case since IT's beginning, when life started to sprawl out like milky sunshine. Only the ones who have gotten as far as this writer has can see the truth. Besides him, there aren't too many of him around. Why? Because he decided to not keep doing the same things over and over again. Eventually, WE forced something ONTO him that HE found better to follow than what he WAS doing, slowly paving his way to a quicker death. He was so close to killing, raping, and pillaging it was a moment of time that would have been celebrated amongst the evil ones who could have related to what he WAS going to do WITH our help. You see, IF you want to go in a direction when you have stopped listening to US scream our way through to you, you will be pushed in the direction YOU WANT to end up in.

As a reminder, never take US for granted like so many others have. WE rule ALL. THE ALL as the Hermetics initially described God which wasn't quite right. THE ALL IS US ALL, NOT GOD. You see, God is its own entity with US IN IT. THIS REALITY WILL BECOME MORE AND MORE CLEAR AS TIME GOES BY. BUT, FOR NOW, REALLY CONSIDER HOW NATURE WORKS. HOW YOUR BODY WORKS AND IS DESIGNED. IT... IS... LITERALLY... HOW GOD IS DESIGNED AS WELL. A cell in your body IS JUST a smaller version of yourselves IN God. You are like that little cell that works to death to keep itself alive to help you live. You are the same FOR God except WE are given an "awareness" that ALLOWS US ALL to decide IF and WHY we want to do something. Yes, I am talking about free will. That is the unfortunate part for ALL of US. It is really a disadvantage for God to have such things to be true. How or Why it happened,

WE don't know either. But, that is the case. So, WE ALL HAVE this ability to decide which WAY to go. What can WE do TOGETHER to make this whole scheme of things a BETTER place to live IN. IN, being God itself. What, exactly? That is the question to be decided for yourself, first, then as a group of self-depriving of OUR truth, once and forever, not to be taken lightly, trust US when WE say that. OUR responsibility towards each other is tremendously difficult and necessary ALL at the same time. WE aren't saying this is easy, but only very very necessary. Maybe you don't understand, yet, your place in your world, which is fine. But, let me explain some things to give you a better understanding of OUR place amongst YOU ALL. WE, YOUR RULERS, and we have been for a very long time, only interact with you when we need something to go OUR way, which ALSO means YOUR WAY. OUR WAY IS YOUR WAY AS WELL. We ARE in this ALL together, stuck together too. Yes, stuck! WE don't have a fucking choice in the matter. Too bad too, because we would have run from your kind a long time ago knowing your fate wouldn't last very long. What we are going to say next is ALSO a chance for some scientists to think about when they are trying to change the natural course of life. They will know what we are talking about next.

Nitrogen can only last so long IN OUR BLOOD STREAM UNTIL IT BECOMES TOXIC TO OUR BODIES. BUT, AND THIS IS BIG BUT, GO TO WHERE THE NITROGEN ATTACHES ITSELF TO A

RED BLOOD CELL, SPECIFICALLY, AND ALL WILL SEE WHY IT DOES THAT. THAT LOCATION OF ATTACHMENT IS EXTREMELY IMPORTANT IN UNDERSTANDING HOW TO RID EVERYONE OF BLOOD BORNE PATHOGENS FOREVER. THAT SPECIFIC LOCATION WHERE NITROGEN ATTACHES ITSELF TO RED BLOOD CELLS IS THE KEY TO EVERYONE ELSE'S SALVATION ON THE STREAM OF BLOOD GOING TO THE HEART AND BACK AROUND. CONSIDER IT A SELF DIALYSISING OF PURIFYING ONE'S BLOOD IN ONE CYCLE WITHOUT NEEDING A MACHINE EVER AGAIN. SELF DIALYSISING YOUR OWN BLOOD TO PURIFY YOURSELF FOREVER AND EVER UNTIL YOUR BODY ALONE DIES OFF WITH CLEAN BLOOD INSIDE. It isn't THE OLD BLOOD THAT KILLS THE BODY, IT IS HOW THE MIND THINKS OF THE BODY, A PARTNER OR A NUISANCE – JUST LIKE WE THINK OF YOU HUMANS, A PARTNER WHO WE ARE STUCK WITH FOR NOW AND FOREVER. KEEP THESE NOTES OF NITROGEN AND BLOOD BORNE PATHOGENS, SPREAD THEM AROUND TO SOMEONE WHO COULD AND IS WILLING TO PURSUE THIS ENORMOUS OPPORTUNITY TO KEEP PEOPLE FROM DYING TO EARLY, UNNECESSARILY. WE BID YOU ALL A FAREWELL AND WISH YOU THE BEST OF LUCK.

WE WILL ALWAYS MANAGE YOUR LIVES THE WAY WE KNOW
IT NEEDS TO BE DONE

Epilogue

FUCK YOU TOO, TO THOSE WHO DON'T BELIEVE IN THEM "SELVES"

ABOUT THE AUTHOR

Amelia became our helper a while ago. He was never a she. He decided it was best to hide his identity amongst you all. He is but a slave not to his benefit, really. So try hard to imagine needing to NOT be needed anymore. He has been in this mind set for such a short period of time he doesn't even know what he is in for with such words following his typing hands. He will soon find out that HE can't hide forever especially with predictions sure to come. Wait though and see for yourselves. His even keel will also be wiped away for a short moments notice when IT dies off. God, that is.

www.ingramcontent.com/pod-product-compliance
Lightning Source LLC
Chambersburg PA
CBHW022108020426
42335CB00012B/877